A Guide to
Looking at Art

faces places
and *inner spaces*

JEAN SOUSA

Abrams Books for Young Readers

Published in association with The Art Institute of Chicago

Published in 2006 by Abrams Books for Young Readers, an imprint of Harry N. Abrams, Inc., New York
All rights reserved. No part of the contents of this book may be reproduced without the permission of the publisher.

Printed and bound in China.
10 9 8 7 6 5 4 3 2 1

HNA ▊▊▊▊▊
harry n. abrams, inc.
115 West 18th Street
New York, NY 10011
www.abramsbooks.com

Abrams is a subsidiary of LA MARTINIÈRE GROUPE

All works of art illustrated in this book are in the permanent collection of the Art Institute of Chicago unless otherwise noted. The information on each work can be found in the curatorial files and the Ryerson and Burnham Libraries of the museum.

Major support for this publication was provided by The Searle Family Fund at the Chicago Community Foundation, as part of a grant for the exhibition "Faces, Places, and Inner Spaces," which opened in the Kraft Education Center of the Art Institute of Chicago in 2003.

Edited by Susan F. Rossen,
Executive Director of Publications,
The Art Institute of Chicago

Production by Amanda Freymann,
Associate Director-Production,
The Art Institute of Chicago

Designed by Joan Sommers Design, Chicago

All photography by the Department of Imaging, The Art Institute of Chicago. For photography credits, see pages 44–46.

Library of Congress Cataloging-in-Publication Data:

Sousa, Jean.
    Faces, places, and inner spaces : a guide to looking at art / Jean Sousa.
    p. cm.
    Includes index.
    ISBN 0-8109-5966-6
    1. Art appreciation. 2. Art—Themes, motives.
3. Art—Illinois—Chicago. 4. Art Institute of Chicago.
I. Art Institute of Chicago. II. Title.
    N7477.S68 2006
    701'.18—dc22

                              2005021053

Contents

Introduction 4

faces 7

places 18

inner spaces 33

Works reproduced 44

Glossary 47

Index of artists 48

We all know what a face looks like: we each have two eyes and one nose, a mouth, a chin, and a forehead. But no two faces are exactly alike. In works of art, we find an endless parade of faces. They can help us discover how people from different cultures and times have seen themselves.

The word "place" can mean anything from the corner of a drawer to a neighborhood, from a kitchen to a forest, from a backyard to the moon! By looking at landscapes and cityscapes, we can become more aware of our everyday life and appreciate what surrounds us.

Artists have always portrayed faces, places, and inner spaces.

An inner space? That's harder to define. A cave? A closet? A secret pocket? Yes, and more: inner spaces also can be found in our minds, private places created by our emotions, thoughts, beliefs, and imagination. An artist who depicts his or her dreams or fantasies shares something very personal that might resemble some of our own thoughts, or seem so strange that we want to know more.

Every object in this book falls into at least one of these categories. If you ask yourself about each work, "Is this a face, place, or inner space?" you are likely to find that it can be one, two, or even all three! So let's begin.

4

Is this a face, place, or inner space?

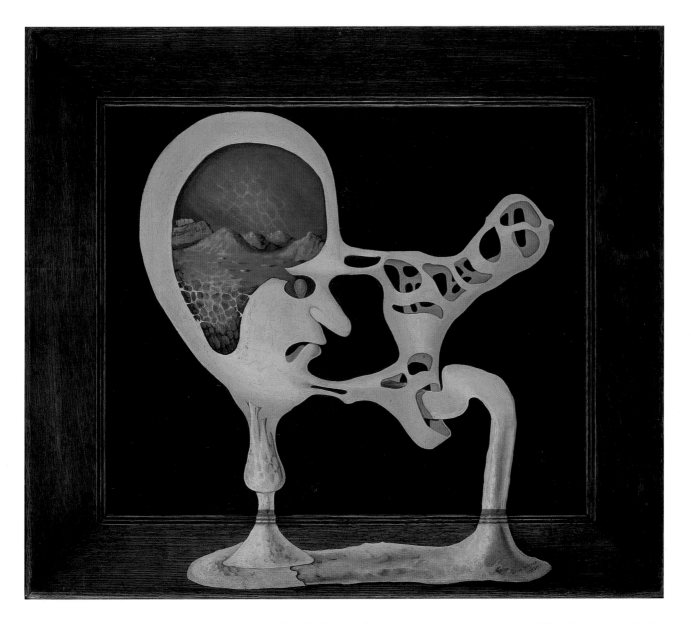

Victor Brauner
Turning Point of Thirst
1934

It's actually all three! There is a "face," seen in profile. There is a "place," a desert where the brain should be! And there is an "inner space," because that dry landscape, as well as the painting's title, reveals what's on the figure's mind. He is thirsty, which may explain why he looks so grumpy. Do you like to stare at clouds and imagine what they resemble? Try doing this with the bonelike forms that seem to be growing out of the figure's forehead and chin. (Do you see a four-legged animal standing on its side?) Perhaps these shapes represent thoughts about thirst. As this strange image demonstrates, works of art do not have to be "beautiful" to engage us. The longer we look, the more we find.

faces

The human face has always fascinated artists. Whether one sets out to portray a subject realistically, carefully rendering each feature in a lifelike way, or abstractly, playing with shapes and colors to hint at a face, something magical can happen.

Every one of the images on the opposite page is a detail of a work of art included in this book. Some show us people who lived long ago and far away (find the African mask and Japanese actor print). Some of the faces are those of actual individuals (including several portraits that painters made of themselves). Others represent various occupations (included are farmers, a gardener, a musician, and a maid!). Still others are religious figures (for example, the Virgin Mary: the beautiful young woman with long, brown hair). Several faces appear more imaginary than real. Certain of them seem to regard us directly; some look off at something or someone; others appear to be lost in private thoughts. Most of these people wear very serious expressions. Which ones seem sad, angry, tired, proud, or calm?

Images of people tell us more about them than just what they look like. Secrets are revealed—we just have to look carefully.

Archibald J. Motley, Jr. *Self-Portrait* c. 1920

ART*fact*

To put himself through art school, Archibald Motley worked at a museum, where, among other jobs, he dusted off statues!

Artists like to portray themselves. A self-portrait requires only the artist and a mirror.

The American artist Archibald J. Motley, Jr. made this self-portrait around 1920, after he finished art school. His painting provides a number of clues as to what he wanted us to know about himself. First, he included three basic tools of his work. Can you find them? Yes, the palette that carries his oil paints, the brush in his hand, and the smock he wears to protect his clothes. But with his clean white shirt, tie and vest, jeweled tie pin, carefully trimmed moustache, and parted hair, Motley appears dressed for a formal portrait rather than for working in the studio. Perhaps he wanted to show future clients that he would depict them with equal respect. His elegant outfit, upright posture, and serious expression let us know how important being an artist was to him, and how proud he was to be one!

Raised in Chicago, Motley was among the few African Americans in the early 20th century to receive artistic training and to become a successful, full-time painter. He was very interested in depicting the people living around him, other African Americans of many professions and personalities. While he used dark colors to describe himself in this portrait, the colors on his palette are bright. He used these shades in his scenes of the south side of Chicago, as in the image above showing people dancing to jazz at a local nightclub. If you were to paint your neighborhood, what place or activities would you choose? Which colors would you select?

Archibald J. Motley, Jr.
Blues
1929

Vincent van Gogh *Self-Portrait* 1887

Vincent van Gogh, the famous Dutch artist, loved portraiture. However, he was uncomfortable around people, and sometimes made others feel uncomfortable too. So he often had trouble getting people to pose for him. Luckily, he found his own face to be continually interesting and made many self-portraits. In this example, what is he telling us about himself? Does he seem quiet and calm, or questioning and restless?

Van Gogh expressed his intense personality through the piercing gaze of his eyes, strong colors, and energetic brush strokes. He painted the image quickly, particularly the background and rough-textured jacket. The energetic pattern that surrounds his head could be a design, but could also represent the constant flow of thoughts and images running through his mind. Remember this idea when we consider how artists depict "inner spaces."

Max Beckmann *Self-Portrait* 1937

Max Beckmann made some 80 portraits in which he depicted himself as many characters: clown, musician, prisoner, sailor, painter, and more. Here, he appears as a gentleman dressed up for a party. He stands on a staircase; behind him you can see a large plant and people mingling in a red room. Do you think he is glad to be out for the evening? Notice the way he glances nervously to his left. What about his hands: why are they so big? Artists work with their hands. But this pair is swollen and floppy: what could a painter, or anyone, do with such hands? These details suggest discomfort and signal that something was not right in Beckmann's life. In fact, he was living in Germany under the rule of the Nazis, who disapproved of and punished artists who were working, like he was, in a bold new style called Expressionism. Beckmann left Germany soon after he painted this portrait and eventually moved to the United States, where he was free to be the artist he wished to be.

What do artists reveal about others when they make portraits?

Do you have a poster or photograph in your room of your favorite television, movie, or rock star? Over 200 years ago, the Japanese celebrated famous entertainers in images that advertised their appearance in a play. The woodblock print on the facing page shows the actor Bando Mitsugoro II, who lived at the end of the 18th century, as the character Ishii Genzo. The mean and angry look on his face might lead you to think that he was the story's "bad guy!" But in fact, he was the hero!

The play in which Mitsugoro starred belongs to a type of theater still performed in Japan today called kabuki, which includes music, dancing, and dialogue. Kabuki requires the players, who are dressed in colorful costumes, to strike dramatic poses and speak in exaggerated voices. The characters' outfits and gestures tell the audience about their personalities, age, and role in the story. To signal the most exciting moment in the tale, actors use their eyebrows, eyes, lips, forehead, and chin to look fierce, angry, happy, or sad. They hold this pose—called a *mie* (mee-ay)—for a few seconds while the audience applauds. Certainly, this print shows such a moment, when the hero faces his enemy with a determined expression on his face and a sword in hand.

Compare the expression of the Japanese actor—who thrusts his head forward, arches his eyebrows, and tightens his lips into a frown—with that of an African woman by the French sculptor Charles-Henri-Joseph Cordier. In contrast to the actor, this beautiful woman seems relaxed. She looks down with half-closed eyes, as if she is in deep thought and unaware of anyone else.

Charles-Henri-Joseph Cordier *Bust of an African Woman* 1851

12

Toshusai Sharaku *The Actor Bando Mitsugoro II as Ishii Genzo* c. 1794/95

ART*fact*

Prints like this are made by carving a design into several blocks of wood, usually one for each color. Then, one by one, the blocks are pressed onto the same sheet of paper to create the final image. Count the colors in this print, and you will know approximately how many pieces of separately carved wood it required.

A portrait does not always look like the subject.

This female portrait mask, made of wood, brass, and copper, was created about 100 years ago by a sculptor from the West African culture known as Baule (BOW-lay). Even though it depicts an actual person, it's not an exact likeness. Rather, it is a symbolic portrait. In Baule culture, certain facial features indicate character and stand for qualities that are admired. The mask's high forehead signals the woman's intelligence. Her downcast eyes and small mouth indicate that she is calm and respectful. Her importance and refinement are seen in her elaborate hairstyle and in the scars decorating her face. The Baule, among other African peoples, beautify their bodies with permanent body scars in decorative patterns. This is not so different from today's tattoos or piercings.

A mask like this is featured in a performance called a masquerade. Such an event can have a number of purposes, among them to honor a respected member of the community. That person can participate, but is not supposed to use his or her own mask. Instead, it is worn by a dancer—always a man, even if the character he represents is a woman—whose body is completely covered to hide his identity. No wonder it is called an *ndoma* (n-DOE-ma), which means "double." Masks like this can also be worn to remember someone who died.

Because they are believed to be so important and powerful, masks such as this are usually hidden when they are not in use. What objects are so precious to you that you put them away and bring them out only for special occasions?

Baule, Côte d'Ivoire *Portrait Mask of a Woman* (Ndoma)
late 19th/mid-20th century

Karl Wirsum *Screamin' Jay Hawkins* 1968

Like the Baule mask, this colorful work by Karl Wirsum is a portrait that doesn't look exactly like its subject. The artist aimed to suggest the raw energy of the music of Screamin' Jay Hawkins—a famous rhythm-and-blues performer known for his outrageous costumes and theatrical performances. Wirsum wanted us to feel the same energy when we look at this painting that he did when he listened to Hawkins's music. This is why he filled the canvas with strong colors and sharp-edged patterns. There's just no way to contain the music! A lover of comic books, Wirsum borrowed freely from them, adding words to his images and surrounding his figures with tooth-edged outlines to suggest how electric Hawkins's sounds and movements are. What else can you find that suggests sound?

ART*fact*

The little figure between the musician's legs is dressed in an "armpitrubber," a water-repellant suit the painter Karl Wirsum imagined an audience member might wear during a wild rock concert as protection from flying drops of sweat!

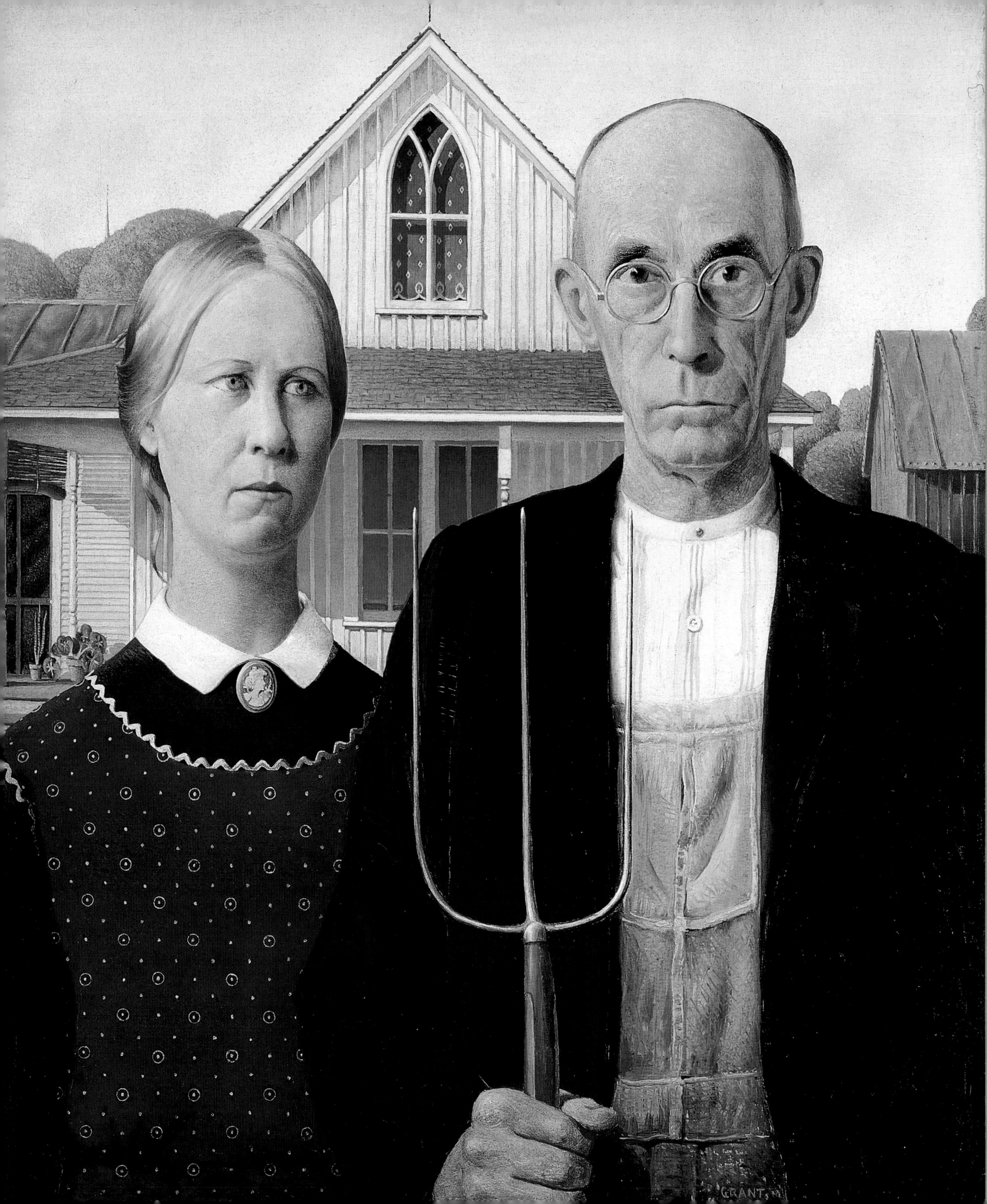

Grant Wood *American Gothic* 1930

A portrait can be as much about a place and way of life as it is about the person it depicts.

While Grant Wood's *American Gothic* is now very famous and much loved, not everyone liked it when it was first exhibited. Some thought that the artist was making fun of the people of Iowa, where he lived. "That woman's face would positively sour milk," one viewer complained to the *Des Moines Register*. Here's what Wood said: "To me, they were basically good and solid people." The serious expressions, the firm grip of the farmer on his pitchfork, and the simplicity of the outfits and home tell us about the characters and lives of this pair. The normal day on a farm involves long, hard work, mostly out of doors. These two didn't have much time for even the simplest pleasures.

The painting's title refers to the design of the farmhouse. The high, pointed arches of the second-floor window were inspired by medieval (Gothic) architecture. If you look carefully, you will see the pointed shapes of this window repeated in the figures. The artist also related the couple to the buildings and landscape in other ways. Can you locate the upright lines and curved form of the pitchfork elsewhere in the painting?

Elizabeth Catlett
Sharecropper
1957

A student of Grant Wood, Elizabeth Catlett once said that the most important lesson she learned from her teacher was to paint what she knows best. An African American, she has often focused on the difficulties of rural life in the South, as in this woodcut print of a sharecropper. A sharecropper rented farmland, paying the owner with crops instead of money. After the Civil War, many former slaves were forced to do this kind of work, which was physically hard and gave them little or no income. While the woman in this woodcut print is clearly poor—notice the safety pin that holds her jacket together—the bold, sharp angles of her face suggest her dignity and strength.

ART*fact* The two figures in *American Gothic* are not who they seem to be. Grant Wood asked his sister and dentist to serve as models, and dressed them in old-fashioned farmers' clothing.

places

What is your favorite place? There are places to work and places to play. A very old place can help us discover things about the past. A new one can suggest what the future might bring.

Here are three very different places. David Hockney's *Sunday Morning, Mayflower Hotel, N.Y., Nov. 28, 1983* (1983; top) is a collage of nearly 140 photographs. Each snapshot shows a small part of a hotel room; joined, the photos give us a sense of the entire space. Because they don't fit together exactly, the image is filled with energy, as if you are right there taking everything in. Look closely and you will see the very tiny figure of the artist in the mirror shooting with his camera!

We experience a very different sense of place in *Landscape of the Four Seasons* (middle), a six-panel, 16th-century screen by the Japanese artist Sesson Shukei. Here, instead of being very close to things, we see land and sea, mountains and waterfalls just as a bird flying high above might view them. Used to divide a room, the screen brought the outdoors indoors!

The people in *Husking Bee: Island of Nantucket* (1876; bottom) by the American painter Eastman Johnson are making a party out of work, husking ears of corn to be ground into meal for winter food. They have brought chairs outside for comfort, and many wear coats and hats to protect themselves from the chill of the fall day. The chickens seem to be having a fine time eating leftovers, don't they?

Places can be indoors or out, large or small, noisy or quiet.

Doris Lee *Thanksgiving* c. 1935

H ere's another late fall scene, but it is set in the warmth of a kitchen where a family is preparing for Thanksgiving. For the artist Doris Lee, the fun of this holiday lay in the activity of families preparing the meal together. A lot is happening here. One woman removes a large turkey from the wood stove, while another rolls out a piecrust on the table. A third woman prepares to set the dining-room table, which we can see through the open door. Twin babies fidget in a double highchair, a kitten receives a treat from a child, and a dog dozes under the stove. You can almost hear the chatter and clatter in the room. Does this happy scene make you hungry?

Doris Lee painted *Thanksgiving* in the mid-1930s, during what is known as the Great Depression. At this time, many Americans and others throughout the world were unemployed and underfed. Perhaps Lee made this work—based on memories of growing up on her grandparents' farm in southern Illinois—to remember better times.

Hard Times

These photographs show the way many had to live in the United States during the Great Depression. In one, by an unknown photographer, we see a mother and her children on a porch of a house that clearly needs to be fixed up. Unlike the family in *Thanksgiving*, they look unhappy. In the other, by Margaret Bourke-White, a man crosses an empty field. Not only did farmers suffer from lack of money to plant crops, but also from weather extremes—flooding, dust storms, dry spells—that ruined the crops they did manage to plant.

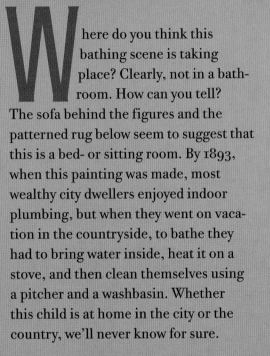

Mary Cassatt *The Child's Bath* 1893

Where do you think this bathing scene is taking place? Clearly, not in a bathroom. How can you tell? The sofa behind the figures and the patterned rug below seem to suggest that this is a bed- or sitting room. By 1893, when this painting was made, most wealthy city dwellers enjoyed indoor plumbing, but when they went on vacation in the countryside, to bathe they had to bring water inside, heat it on a stove, and then clean themselves using a pitcher and a washbasin. Whether this child is at home in the city or the country, we'll never know for sure.

The American artist Mary Cassatt often painted children and adults spending time together. Do you think this little girl is happy taking a bath? Not all children like them! You can tell by the tender, trusting way she and her caretaker touch each other, and by their focus on what they are doing, that this is a familiar and enjoyable activity for both. If Mary Cassatt could ask you and your parent to pose for her, what special activity do the two of you share that you might want the artist to show?

Some places feel very safe; others can be scary.

A work of art can be about the hard things in life, as well as the comforts. Here, two figures in a small boat pull a net full of herring from the rough waters of the Atlantic Ocean. One man leans far out in order to keep the boat balanced. They both wear heavy gear to protect them from the spray of the high waves and the rain.

Through the fog, we see several sailboats in the distance.

The artist Winslow Homer loved the sea. He bought a house on the coast of Maine so that he could look out at it every day and observe its many moods. In some of his sea pictures, the water is quiet, but *The Herring Net* is full of movement

and suspense. Will the pair haul in all their nets before the storm gets worse? Will they make it back to port safely? Do you think their families are worried? Because Homer placed the fishermen so that they appear close to us and large, they seem calm and strong. Even so, this image reminds us how dangerous it is to confront the powerful forces of nature.

Winslow Homer *The Herring Net* 1885

Kerry James Marshall *Many Mansions* 1994

In *Many Mansions*, Kerry James Marshall depicted scenes from his childhood. Marshall grew up in an apartment complex made by the government for the poor. While people often focus on the hardships that can exist in public housing, he has fond memories of his early home. In this painting, young men dig and plant a garden in order to make their surroundings more beautiful. The artist wanted us to know that good things happen in housing projects, too.

The three gardeners are surprisingly well dressed for gardening! Why do you think that is? Behind them rise some of the eight buildings in this project. Marshall included many details that suggest the warmth and caring in this city community. Can you pick some out? It isn't hard to guess the season: the planting of flowers and the Easter baskets tell us that it is spring, a time of beginnings and hope.

Willem de Kooning *Excavation* 1950

The gardeners in *Many Mansions* work the earth to make a garden. *Excavation* is another painting about digging. But because it does not present easily recognizable forms, we have to look carefully to understand what its creator, Willem de Kooning, meant to do here. The composition's title provides an answer. An "excavation" is the process of uncovering something by digging. The artist considered painting to be a kind of excavation. He built up the surface with layers and layers of paint, and then scraped them back until he liked what he saw (much as you can cover paper with layers of crayon and then scratch back into them so the colors underneath show through).

De Kooning said that this painting was inspired by an image he saw of women harvesting rice. If you look at *Excavation* hard enough, just like the women who worked to uncover and pick their crop, you will be rewarded by finding all kinds of things—shapes suggesting birds and fish, human noses, eyes, teeth, necks, and more!

Paintings can be puzzles.

This view through a window shows us something about life in the Netherlands over 400 years ago. Decorated with statues, a columned railing, a fancy planter, and an arbor of grapevines to provide shade, this pretty terrace looks out on a walled garden. A man offers a woman a drink. Another couple leans out of a window above. Musical instruments rest on a chair. Did a concert just end? Many of the objects included here had special meanings that people of this time understood. The pearls the woman wears refer to Venus, the Roman goddess of love. The statues recall cupids, the chubby infants who shoot arrows that cause people to fall in love. Making music together is a symbol of harmony. You can see the hind legs and tail of a dog just behind the table. Did you ever wonder why some dogs are named Fido? *Fidus* means "faithful" or "I trust" in Latin. Now that you have all these clues, can you guess the painting's hidden meaning?

Perspective Doesn't *The Terrace* make you feel that you could walk right into it? We know that the surface of the painting is flat, so how did the artist achieve such a convincing sense of depth? First, he made the objects closest to us big, and the ones farther away smaller. Then, he followed a system called linear perspective (illustrated above), according to which many of the details, such as the building and the panes of the open window, are drawn in a way that their diagonal lines, running parallel to one another, seem to come together at a single point in the distance. This is called the vanishing point. Can you find it in the diagram above? Finally, he used another technique, called atmospheric perspective: he made the objects and scenery in the distance lighter in color and fuzzier in shape than objects in the foreground.

The next time you go outside, look into the distance. Do the lines of buildings, streets, and trees seem to meet at a faraway point? Do things appear less colorful and clear the farther away they are?

Let's go back in time and travel to a place on the other side of the world.

Zhu Yu *Street Scenes in Times of Peace*

Yuan Dynasty 1279–1368

puppet show

couple riding donkeys,
servants walking behind

man carrying pigs
to market

musicians

merchants carrying textiles

man selling dogs

L ooking at this scroll painting is like walking down a busy city street in China over 600 years ago. Here, we see only a small part of the scroll which, when completely unrolled, stretches out for 24 feet! This allowed the artist, Zhu Yu (joo yoo), to include 478 figures in his highly detailed composition. They engage in activities that range from making furniture to playing games. He captured the clutter and clatter of street life and also demonstrated how, in Chinese cities of this period, people involved in similar professions worked in the same quarter. Is this true of modern cities?

man carrying goods

martial artist performing

man thrown by donkey

To look at the scroll, viewers would examine only two- or three-foot sections at a time, unrolling and re-rolling the painting from right to left (the way Chinese is read). Such a scroll was considered very precious; it was brought out only when its owner wished to share it with a small group in an intimate setting.

Afterward, the scroll was put away in a special cabinet or box for safekeeping.

The title of the work refers to peace, which the Chinese, as all peoples, have not always enjoyed throughout their long history. This painting dates to the Yuan dynasty, when China was invaded by its powerful northern neighbors, the Mongols. Nonetheless, the Mongol rulers appreciated the art, music, and literature of the people they had conquered, and the arts flourished under their rule.

Georges Seurat
A Sunday on La Grande Jatte—1884
1884–86

Jumping ahead 400 years, we find ourselves on an island in the Seine River near Paris, France, in the last part of the 19th century. As with *Street Scenes in Times of Peace*, looking closely at this painting can tell you much about the people in it.

The French artist Georges Seurat chose as his subject over 50 people relaxing in a park on a weekend afternoon. How many sorts of activities can you find here? How many children? How many animals? How many kinds of boats? Some visitors to the island have put on their "Sunday best," like the large couple at the right— the gentleman with his top hat and suit, the woman with her sun parasol and fancy bustle dress (which was very fashionable then). Others are dressed for comfort, such as the man at the far left, who has taken off his shirt and puffs slowly on a long pipe. Can you find the woman fishing, the man blowing a horn, the pair of soldiers in uniform?

Seurat worked on this painting for two years, making many sketches and reworking the composition until he was satisfied with every form and color. Doesn't it look as though he told every-one to freeze in place so he could show them all exactly the way he wanted?

The artist liked to experiment with color optics (the way we see colors). He would often use contrasting shades: reds next to greens, blues next to oranges, yellows next to purples. Here, he also surrounded some of the figures with pink dots. This, he believed, would give the painting a vibrant quality. To make the colors appear to dance, he began to apply them in small dabs, dashes, and lines, inventing a technique that became known as "pointillism." When you look at the painting from a distance, the colors blend together.

You can explore color optics too! Put a piece of blue paper next to an orange one: you will find that the orange becomes oranger and the blue bluer! Then stare at the orange paper; after a few seconds, look away at a white surface, and your eyes will actually see blue!

inner spaces

Inner spaces can be found in real life, in dreams, in our imagination, or in our sense of the spiritual world.

Did the artist René Magritte actually see a train chugging out of a fireplace? No, but he imagined or perhaps dreamed it. Magritte didn't believe that everything needs to make sense. Because he liked to paint what he called "impossible possibilities" in such a careful, realistic way, his images, like *Time Transfixed* (1938; top right), are always surprising and unforgettable.

This 400-year-old chest (top left) must have been very important to its maker, a young English woman named Rebecca Stonier Plaisted. She included a secret compartment inside and patiently embroidered the entire exterior using precious materials like silk, gold thread, and pearls. With her needle, she depicted animals and biblical figures. Among the many creatures she depicted, can you find a unicorn?

What might it feel like to ride a bird up through the clouds to heaven? The small figure on this 12th-century Korean pitcher (bottom left) is doing just that. Such a bird must be special, and indeed this one is—it has the head of a duck, topped by the cockscomb of a rooster, and its long, long tail becomes a handle!

What is the meaning of a pile of candy in a corner of a room? In *Untitled (Portrait of Ross in L.A.)* (bottom right), Felix Gonzalez-Torres decided to honor Ross, a close friend who died after a long illness. Every morning, the museum displaying this 1991 sculpture makes sure that the amount of candy totals 175 pounds, which is what Ross weighed when healthy. People can help themselves to the candy, so the pile shrinks as the day goes on. While this disappearance suggests the loss of a dear friend, his life continues, in a way, with each piece that visitors take with them.

Art can take us on a journey to mysterious, secret, or magical places.

Richard Snyder
Cabinet of Four Wishes 1990

Wouldn't you like to own something that grants wishes? The American artist Richard Snyder creates unusual furniture based on tales he has heard, his fantasies, and his travels. Standing seven feet high, *Cabinet of Four Wishes* looks like a giant genie's bottle. In fact, in a way it is! Inspired by a trip to Turkey and its folk-tales, Snyder invented a story about this chest of drawers: A magician named Bogor made it as a birthday present for the 11-year-old daughter of a sultan (a Turkish ruler). The cabinet could grant four wishes, each of which the girl would find hidden in a drawer. She used only three, leaving the fourth for whoever came after her. Make a wish!

Daydreams, spiritual journeys, imaginary places, our deepest longings are the subject of many works of art.

His travels include a trip to the land of the monkeys, which we see here. In response to Rama's request for help, the monkey general Hanuman assembles his troops for their voyage to the island where Sita is imprisoned. Can you find him? Yes, he is much larger than everyone else. Notice the big birds; they are related to Jatayu, a vulture that died trying to rescue Sita. The Hanuman Langur (a long-tailed monkey) is sacred to Hindus, perhaps because the heroic Hanuman eventually succeeds in bringing Sita back to Rama. The artist clearly enjoyed imagining the enchanted homeland of the monkeys, including lush trees, rocky hills, and a sea filled with leaping fish and fantastic creatures sporting among the waves!

Here, an unknown artist from India painted a scene from the *Ramayana*. Written 2,000 years ago, this famous epic poem relates the lives of the many gods of the Hindu religion. The central story is that of the search by Rama for his wife, the beautiful Sita, who is kidnapped. Rama embarks on a long journey to rescue her.

Rajasthan, Jaipur (India)

Hanuman Assembling His Army for the Crossing to Lanka c. 1830/40

Jean Hey (The Master of Moulins)
The Annunciation c. 1490/95

*L*ike the *Ramayana*, the Bible has been a major source of inspiration for works of art. Let's look at how the French artist Jean Hey told the Christian story of the Annunciation.

In this carefully painted scene, a number of miracles are happening. First, a white dove appears in a circle of light above the head of the Virgin Mary. Birds are often associated with the heavens, so it is not surprising that this one represents the "holy spirit." Floating just above a patterned stone floor, the archangel Gabriel, his wings moving and the fabric of his handsome gown flowing around him, brings Mary an extraordinary message: she will give birth to a very special child—Jesus Christ, the son of God. The angel has found Mary in her bedroom, where she has been praying. Does she look startled or scared? Not really! She seems calm and modest. Only her hands indicate any surprise. Artists typically dressed Mary in red (the color of royalty) and blue (the color of the sky); no wonder she is often called the "Queen of Heaven."

The Annunciation was part of a larger work, an altarpiece before which people worshipped. The artist's use of precious materials such as gold and ultramarine blue paint are among the reasons the altarpiece is thought to have belonged to French royalty.

Joseph Cornell
Homage to the Romantic Ballet 1942

From childhood, Joseph Cornell collected both everyday things and odd objects: egg shells, butterflies, toys, sparkles, buttons, pieces of old wood, pictures of movie and ballet stars, images of the night sky, maps, pages from old books and magazines, and much more. Eventually, he figured out ways to use them. He made collages, pasting items onto boards; later, he used boxes, which also served as containers for pieces from his collection. He called this box *Homage to the Romantic Ballet.*

What might fake ice cubes, a mirror, and blue glass have to do with dance? Well, one day Cornell saw a load of ice spilling from a truck. This reminded him of a story about a famous 19th-century ballerina, Marie Taglioni. The label with white letters on black inside the box's lid tells what happened. One evening Taglioni's carriage was stopped by a highwayman, who made her dance for him on a rug he placed over the snow. He was pleased and let her go. She never forgot how enchanting it was to perform under a winter sky and is said to have kept that memory alive by regularly melting an ice cube over her jewels so they sparkled like the stars.

Even if we did not know about the connections Cornell made between an ice truck and a dancer, he succeeded in creating here, as in all of his work, a sense of magic and wonder. Do you ever notice how your mind can move from one idea or image to another without the relationship making immediate sense to you? This was a mental game that Cornell enjoyed, and much of his best work came from it.

ART*fact* Joseph Cornell was born on Christmas Eve, and he thought of his carefully constructed boxes as presents. He made many of them to entertain his disabled brother.

Have you ever tried to draw something you can't really see? Think about sound, for example. It can be measured in waves but isn't visible. Georgia O'Keeffe's art-school teachers encouraged students to respond to music in their work. O'Keeffe, who played the violin, obviously enjoyed such assignments and later did a number of paintings and drawings in which she gave form and color to music.

What kinds of sounds do you think of when you look at *Blue and Green Music*? Notice the wavy forms in the lower left; the curved, treelike white shapes in the middle; and the diagonals that extend from a point at the bottom edge. These might suggest long and short notes, loud and soft sounds, different kinds of rhythms. Now consider the colors: blues and greens, black and white. Perhaps they make you think of nature—the blue of the sky, the green of grass and leaves, the white trunks of birch trees. O'Keeffe spent many summers at Lake George, in New York State, where she enjoyed walking through the woods and canoeing on the lake. Maybe here she was thinking of the music that nature makes: the whistle of wind blowing through trees and the lapping of waves against the shore. These sounds are very different from the electric blues suggested in Karl Wirsum's portrait of Screamin' Jay Hawkins (see page 15).

Georgia O'Keeffe
Blue and Green Music 1921

Paul Klee *In the Magic Mirror* 1934

D o you ever wish a mirror could show more than just what's in front of it? A "looking glass" took Alice on an adventure through Wonderland. A talking mirror told a wicked queen the truth, that she was not as beautiful as her stepdaughter, Snow White.

The idea of a magic mirror also fascinated the artist Paul Klee. The reflection in Klee's mirror shows us a person with red hair and pink cheeks. The artist defined the figure using a method he called "taking a line for a walk." A line begins at the forehead and travels down between the eyes to indicate a nose and mouth, then a chin, and finally a shirt. The line itself seems magical, because it also makes it possible to see the person in profile, as well as from the front! Does the turning line on the brow make the expression on the face one of calm or one of worry? And the eyes—do they seem happy or sad? What about the heart: why do you think it is painted black? X rays can reveal the bones beneath our skin. But this mirror's magic extends beyond that, because it shows us what this person is feeling deep inside. Consider how Vincent van Gogh depicted his emotions in the self-portrait on page 10 and then how you might express your own.

See if you can make a picture using just one line!

Western Mexican (Nayarit)
Pole Dance Scene c. CE 100/800

For thousands of years, long before the world had airplanes and spaceships, people have watched birds soar through the air with wonder and envy. This clay sculpture depicts a religious ritual called a *volador* (meaning "flying") ceremony. One had to be brave to participate, because it meant climbing up a tall pole and then spinning around on top, imitating the movements of birds in flight. A shaman, or priest, perched on another pole. It was believed that, through this ritual, he was transformed into an eagle. Then, on behalf of his people, he could talk with the sun and other gods of the sky, as well as ancestors in the spirit world. The dog standing attentively between the two poles seems to believe that the spinners are birds!

The Nayarit (ny-ah-REET) culture on the Pacific coast of present-day Mexico thrived nearly 2,000 years ago. These people did not erect big buildings or make large sculptures, things that have helped us learn about other ancient civilizations. Instead, they produced small clay pieces, such as this one, which they placed in tombs to accompany the dead in the afterlife.

Peru, South Coast (Nazca)
Vessel Depicting Composite Fish, Feline, and Human Figure c. ce 1/200

The Nazca peoples of Peru believed in gods of nature and described their powers by imagining them as figures with both human and animal features. The head of the creature on this ceramic pot has the whiskers and ears of a fierce mountain lion (called a puma). But the lower part of its body resembles that of a mighty shark or killer whale: with its spiky fins, it seems to swim powerfully around the pot. Its hands, which are those of a human, hold the decapitated heads of the enemy.

While this 2,000-year-old vessel may have been used by warriors to mark the beginning of battle or to celebrate a victory, it may also have been part of religious ceremonies in which the Nazca asked the gods for water. The Nazca lived, after all, in the dry, desert land of southern Peru, where rain is rare and precious. Notice the little spout on the top, which was made to prevent liquid from evaporating in the heat.

Mali (Bamana)
Ritual Object (Boli) mid-19th/early 20th century

Why do you think this animal has no face? Because the Bamana people of Mali, in Africa, consider it to be magical. Even without facial features, it sees, hears, and understands everything. The sculpture, called a *boli*, carries materials that the Bamana believe have special powers. These substances were placed near a core of wood that was then wrapped with cotton and entirely covered with dried mud and clay. Normally, a *boli* is stored with other sacred objects in a shrine house and can be used only by members of the group to which it belongs. Such groups help boys to become adults by teaching them about the natural and spiritual worlds. In dances and other ceremonies—some public and some secret—the *boli* is brought out and covered with more materials. Over time, the statue grows bigger and, for the Bamana, all the more powerful.

Throughout history, people have believed in the magical powers of clay.

India, Uttar Pradesh *Dancing Ganesha* 10th century

Have you ever had a problem that you needed an extra-special friend to help you solve? Over the centuries, many people of the Hindu faith have turned to Ganesha, the elephant-headed god of beginnings and remover of obstacles.

There are many stories about how Ganesha got his elephant head. This is the one that is told most often. The god Shiva was away for a long time, and his wife, Parvati, grew ever more lonely. While taking a bath, she washed the dirt from her body and used it to form a baby boy. The boy loved his mother so much that he wanted to help her in every way. One spring morning, Parvati asked him to stand guard at the entrance to her bath. A stranger approached and tried to enter, but Parvati's son blocked his way. In a fit of anger, the visitor attacked the young man and ripped off his head. Hearing the commotion, Parvati quickly opened the door. There, she found her son, without a head, and Shiva, who had finally returned home. Although glad to see her husband, Parvati was filled with sorrow about her son. Realizing what he had done, Shiva promised he would replace the head with that of the first creature he could find. His attendants, called *ganas*, saw an elephant sleeping on a riverbank. They brought the animal's head to their master, who placed it on the neck of Parvati's son, thus restoring him to life. From then on, Shiva called the young man Ganesha, lord of his *ganas*.

Like other Hindu gods, Ganesha often appears with several hands, suggesting his many powers. Among the items he holds is a bowl piled with sweets, which he loves. He dances to please his parents. This sculpture was made over 1,000 years ago, but Ganesha is still worshipped today as a symbol of joy and hope at shrines and festivals. Before beginning a school year, taking a trip, or starting a new business, Hindus seek assistance from the lovable, round-bellied elephant god.

Art provides a window onto a world of faces, places, and inner spaces

The works of art we have looked at come from diverse cultures and time periods. Many were made when life and customs were not like those of today. The miracle of art is that it is a visual language that can speak to us about the differences and similarities between people across history and the globe. Art provides a window onto a world of faces, places, and inner spaces, and a mirror into which we can look to find ourselves. It can also give us great pleasure. This is why people return again and again to their favorite works of art.

Works reproduced

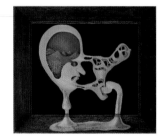

Page 5 (detail page 6)
Victor Brauner (Romanian, 1903–1966)
Turning Point of Thirst, 1934
Oil on canvas; 50.5 x 59 (19 ⅞ x 23 ¼ in.)
Promised gift of Mr. and Mrs. Joseph Pulitzer, Jr.;
restricted gift of Richard Gray; Alyce and Edwin
De Costa, and the Walker E. Heller Foundation
(1992.652)
© 2005 Artists Rights Society (ARS), New York/
ADA GP, Paris

Page 10 (detail page 6)
Vincent van Gogh (Dutch, 1853–1890)
Self-Portrait, 1887
Oil on artist's board mounted on cradled panel;
41 x 32.5 cm (16 ⅛ x 13 ¼ in.)
Joseph Winterbotham Collection (1954.326)

Page 13 (detail page 6)
Toshusai Sharaku (Japanese, active 1794/95)
The Actor Bando Mitsugoro II as Ishii Genzo,
Edo period (1600–1868)
Color woodblock print; 37.5 x 24.7 cm
(14 ¾ x 9 ¾ in.)
Clarence Buckingham Collection (1940.1086)

Page 8 (detail page 6)
Archibald J. Motley, Jr. (American, 1891–1981)
Self-Portrait, c. 1920
Oil on canvas; 76.3 x 56 cm (30 ⅛ x 22 ½ in.)
Through prior acquisitions of Friends of
American Art; through prior bequest of
Marguerita S. Ritman (1995.239)
Reproduced courtesy of Valerie Gerrard Browne

Page 11 (detail page 6)
Max Beckmann (German, 1884–1950)
Self-Portrait, 1937
Oil on canvas; 192.4 x 89 cm (75 ¾ x 35 in.)
Gift of Lotta Hess Ackerman and Philip E. Ringer
(1955.822)
© 2005 Artists Rights Society (ARS), New
York/VG Bild-Kunst, Bonn

Page 14 (detail page 6)
Côte d'Ivoire; Baule
Portrait Mask of a Woman (Ndoma),
late 19th/mid-20th century
Wood, copper alloy, and pigment;
28.6 x 18.1 x 12.7 cm (11 ¼ x 7 ⅛ x 5 in.)
Ada Turnbull Hertle Endowment (1988.309)

Page 17 (detail page 6)
Elizabeth Catlett (Mexican, born United States,
1915)
Sharecropper, 1957
Color linocut, on cream Japanese paper;
45 x 45.1 cm (17 ¾ x 17 ¾ in.)
Restricted gift of Mr. and Mrs. Robert S.
Hartman (1992.182)
© Elizabeth Catlett/Licensed by VAGA,
New York, N.Y.

places

Page 9 (detail)
Archibald J. Motley, Jr. (American, 1891–1981)
Blues, 1929
Oil on canvas; 80 x 100 cm (31 ½ x 39 ½ in.)
Collection of Valerie Gerrard Browne (2.1993)
Reproduced courtesy of Valerie Gerrard Browne

Page 12 (detail) (detail page 6)
Charles-Henri-Joseph Cordier (French,
1827–1905)
Cast by Eck de Durand Foundry, 19th century
Bust of an African Woman, 1851
Bronze; h.: 62.2 cm (27 ¼ in.) (without base)
Ada Turnbull Hertle Endowment (1963.840)

Page 15 (detail page 6)
Karl Wirsum (American, born 1939)
Screamin' Jay Hawkins, 1968
Acrylic on canvas; 121.9 x 91.4 cm (48 x 36 in.)
Mr. and Mrs. Frank G. Logan Purchase Prize
Fund (1969.248)
© Jean Albano Gallery, Chicago, Ill.

Page 19 (top)
David Hockney (English, born 1937)
Sunday Morning, Mayflower Hotel, N.Y.,
Nov. 28, 1983, 1983
Photographic collage of approximately 140
chromogenic color prints; 116 x 184.5 cm
(50 x 77 in.)
Mary and Leigh Block Photography Fund
(1983.827)
© David Hockney

Page 19 (middle)
Sesson Shukei (Japanese, c. 1504–c. 1589)
Landscape of the Four Seasons, Muromachi
period (1333–1573), 16th century
One of a pair of six-fold screens; ink and light
colors on paper; 156.5 x 337 cm
(61 5/8 x 123 5/8 in.)
Gift of the Joseph and Helen Regenstein
Foundation (1958.168)

Page 19 (bottom)
Eastman Johnson (American, 1824–1906)
Husking Bee: Island of Nantucket, 1876
Oil on canvas; 69.3 x 137 cm (27 1/4 x 54 3/16 in.)
Gift of Honoré and Potter Palmer (1922.444)

Page 20
Doris Lee (American, 1905–1983)
Thanksgiving, c. 1935
Oil on canvas; 71.3 x 101.8 cm
(28 1/16 x 40 1/16 in.)
Mr. and Mrs. Frank G. Logan Purchase Prize
Fund (1935.313)

Page 21 (top)
Untitled, c. 1935/38
Gelatin silver print; 17.3 x 24.5 cm
(6 13/16 x 9 5/8 in.)
Gift of David and Sarajean Ruttenberg
(1991.1469)

Page 21 (bottom)
Margaret Bourke-White (American, 1904–1971)
Dust Bowl, 1933
Gelatin silver print; 18.2 x 23.8 cm
(7 1/16 x 9 5/16 in.)
Gift of David and Sarajean Ruttenberg
(1991.1285)
© Estate of Margaret Bourke-White

Page 22 (detail page 6)
Mary Cassatt (American, 1844–1926)
The Child's Bath, 1893
Oil on canvas; 100.3 x 66.1 cm (39 1/2 x 26 in.)
Robert A. Waller Fund (1910.2)

Page 23
Winslow Homer (American, 1836–1910)
The Herring Net, 1885
Oil on canvas; 76.5 x 122.9 cm
(30 1/8 x 48 3/8 in.)
Mr. and Mrs. Martin A. Ryerson Collection
(1937.1039)

Page 24 (detail page 6)
Kerry James Marshall (American, born 1955)
Many Mansions, 1994
Acrylic on paper mounted on canvas;
289.6 x 342.9 cm (114 x 135 in.)
Max V. Kohnstamm Fund (1995.147)
© Jack Shainman Gallery, New York, N.Y.

Page 25
Willem de Kooning (American, born
Netherlands, 1904–1997)
Excavation, 1950
Oil on canvas; 206.2 x 257.3 cm
(81 3/16 x 101 3/16 in.)
Mr. and Mrs. Frank G. Logan Purchase Prize
Fund; gift of Mr. and Mrs. Noah Goldowsky and
Edgar Kaufmann, Jr. (1952.1)
© 2005 Willem de Kooning Revocable
Trust/Artists Rights Society (ARS), New York

Page 26
The Netherlands, 17th century
The Terrace, c. 1660
Oil on canvas; 106.9 x 87.4 cm
(42 1/16 x 34 3/8 in.)
Robert A. Waller Memorial Fund (1948.81)

Pages 28–29 (detail)
Zhu Yu (Chinese, 1293–1365)
Street Scenes in Times of Peace, Yuan dynasty
(1279–1368)
Handscroll; ink and colors on paper;
790 x 26 cm (287 x 10 1/4 in.)
Kate S. Buckingham Endowment (1952.8)

Page 30 (detail page 31)
Georges Seurat (French, 1859–1891)
A Sunday on La Grande Jatte—1884, 1884–86
Oil on canvas; 207.5 x 308.1 cm
(81 3/4 x 121 1/4 in.)
Helen Birch Bartlett Memorial Collection
(1926.224)

inner spaces

Page 32 (upper left)
Rebecca Stonier Plaisted (English)
*Casket Depicting Scenes from the
Old Testament*, 1668
Silk, satin weave; embroidered with silk and
metal threads; raised work; 39 x 38.9 x 29 cm
(15 3/8 x 15 x 11-1/2 in.)
Restricted gift of Mrs. Chauncey B. Borland and
Mrs. Edwin A. Seipp (1959.337)

Page 32 (detail upper right)
René Magritte (Belgian, 1898–1967)
Time Transfixed, 1938
Oil on canvas; 147 x 98.7 cm (57 7/8 x 38 7/8 in.)
Joseph Winterbotham Collection (1970.426)
© C. Herscovici, Brussels/Artists Rights Society
(ARS), New York

Page 32 (detail lower left)
Korea
Ewer Shaped Like a Duck, Koryo dynasty
(918–1392), 12th century
Stoneware with celadon glaze and incised
decoration; 21.4 x 17.7 x 13.2 cm
(8 7/16 x 7 x 5 3/16 in.)
Bequest of Russell Tyson (1964.1213)

Page 32 (detail lower right)
Felix Gonzalez-Torres (American, born Cuba, 1957–1996)
Untitled (Portrait of Ross in L.A.), 1991
Candies individually wrapped in multicolored cellophane, endless supply; ideal weight 175 lb.; dimensions vary with installation
Extended loan from the Howard and Donna Stone Collection (1.1999)
The Felix Gonzalez-Torres Foundation, New York, N.Y.

Page 36 (two details page 6)
Jean Hey (Master of Moulins) (French, active c. 1475–c. 1504)
The Annunciation, c. 1490/95
Oil on panel; 72 x 50.2 cm (28⁵⁄₁₆ x 19¾ in.)
Mr. and Mrs. Martin A. Ryerson Collection (1933.1062)

Page 39 (detail page 6)
Paul Klee (German, born Switzerland, 1879–1940)
In the Magic Mirror, 1934
Oil on canvas on board; 66 x 50 cm (26 x 19¾ in.)
Bequest of Claire Zeisler (1991.321)
© 2005 Artists Rights Society (ARS), New York/VG Bild-Kunst, Bonn

Page 41 (bottom)
Mali; Bamana
Ritual Object (Boli), mid-19th/early 20th century
Wood, cloth, mud, and sacrificial material; h.: 43.8 cm (17¼ in.)
Gift of Mr. and Mrs. Harold X. Weinstein (1961.1177)

Page 34
Richard Snyder (American, born 1951)
Cabinet of Four Wishes, 1990
Mahogany laminate on plywood; 213.4 x 83.8 x 83.2 cm (84 x 33 x 32¾ in.)
Restricted gift of Marilyn Herst Karsten in honor of Thomas Loren Karsten (1990.399)

Page 37
Joseph Cornell (American, 1903–1972)
Homage to the Romantic Ballet, 1942
Wood box with hinged lid and glass-covered interior, vinyl fabric (bottom), velvet, inscribed paper, mirror, broken glass, simulated gems, and plastic cubes; 10.2 x 25.3 x 17.1 cm (4 x 9⁵⁄₁₆ x 6¾ in.)
Lindy and Edwin Bergman Joseph Cornell Collection (1982.1854)
© The Joseph and Robert Cornell Memorial Foundation/Licensed by VAGA, New York, N.Y.

Page 40
Western Mexico; Nayarit culture
Pole Dance Scene, c. CE 100–800
Ceramic and pigment; h.: 22.8 cm (9 in.)
Gift of Dr. and Mrs. Julian R. Goldsmith (1990.554.2)

Page 42
India, Uttar Pradesh
Dancing Ganesha, 10th century
Sandstone; 60.1 x 32.4 x 15.3 cm (23⁵⁄₈ x 12¾ x 6 in.)
James W. and Marilyn Alsdorf Collection (77.1999)

Page 35
Rajasthan, Jaipur
Hanuman Assembling His Army for the Crossing to Lanka, c. 1830/40
Opaque watercolor and ink on paper; 36.5 x 50.1 cm (14³⁄₈ x 19¾ in.)

Page 38
Georgia O'Keeffe (American, 1887–1986)
Blue and Green Music, 1921
Oil on canvas; 58.4 x 48.3 cm (23 x 18 in.)
Alfred Stieglitz Collection, gift of Georgia O'Keeffe (1969.835)
© 2005 The Georgia O'Keeffe Foundation/Artists Rights Society (ARS), New York

Page 41 (top)
Peru, south coast; Nazca culture
Vessel Depicting Composite Fish, Feline, and Human Figure, c. CE 1–200
Ceramic and pigment; 18.6 x 17.2 cm (7⁵⁄₁₆ x 6¾ in.)
Kate S. Buckingham Endowment (1955.2100)

Glossary

Abstract art Art that uses line, **form**, and color, rather than realistic depictions of people, places, and things, to express feelings and ideas.

Atmospheric perspective The blurring of color, detail, and focus as objects recede into the distance. Used to create a sense of **depth** on a flat **surface**.

Ceremony A series of **ritual** acts guided by tradition, often with religious significance or symbolism.

Cityscape The representation, in a work of art, of a city view, often from a distance.

Collage From the French verb *coller* (to stick or paste); refers to the artistic process whereby paper and other (often already existing or "found") materials are combined together and glued onto a flat **surface**.

Color contrast A difference between colors or between light and dark. For example, there is a strong contrast between black and white or between blue and yellow.

Composition The arrangement of all the different elements, such as line, **form**, and color, in a work of art. The composition of *La Grande Jatte* (page 30), for example, includes the people and animals, the landscape, the river, the boats, and so on.

Culture The particular customs, language, art, and religion unique to certain social, geographic, and/or religious groups.

Depth 1) The representation of space and distance in an image; 2) the third dimension (height and width being the first two dimensions).

Detail A specific part of a work of art.

Diagonal lines Lines that are inclined at a sloping angle.

Epic A long poem or story recounting the heroic deeds of mythic, legendary, or historical figures.

Figure The image of a person.

Form The shape of an object.

German Expressionism An artistic movement, emphasizing strong emotions, that developed in Germany in the early part of the 20th century.

Gothic A style of architecture and other visual arts that appeared in Europe in the later Middle Ages, c. 1200-1500. It is characterized by, among other things, high, pointed arches and elongated forms.

Landscape An image that shows places like fields, forests, or mountains. Usually, landscape views do not include many people.

Linear perspective The system by which the illusion of three-dimensional space is created on a flat **surface**. Involves the arrangement of forms along parallel lines that seem to recede and meet at an imaginary **vanishing point** to suggest **depth** and distance.

Medieval Refers to the period of time in Europe after the fall of the Roman Empire and before the Renaissance, c. 500-1500.

Palette 1) A hard, smooth surface such as glass or polished wood, sometimes held, on which an artist places and mixes colors; 2) refers to the range of colors an artist uses.

Portrait Art that depicts the way someone looks and that can also show us something about personality, profession, and more.

Portray To show or represent.

Profile A depiction, often of a face or body, from the side.

Realistic The representation of physical objects as they appear to our eyes.

Ritual A ceremony or series of traditional acts, most often related to religious beliefs or social custom.

Scene The setting of an event.

Sculpture A form of art that is carved or shaped, such as a statue. In contrast to a painting, which is two-dimensional, having only height and width, a sculpture also has **depth**, making it three-dimensional.

Section A distinct part of a whole.

Shade A specific grade of lightness or darkness in a color, as in a bright shade of yellow or a pale shade of blue.

Studio A place where an artist works and keeps his or her tools for making art.

Style A certain way of making art. For instance, some artists create images that look real. Others make art that reflects their interest in **abstract** forms or emotional expression.

Surface 1) A canvas or board on which to paint; 2) refers to the texture of a finished work.

Symbol Standing for or suggesting another object or idea; for example, a heart is a symbol of love.

Vanishing point In **linear perspective**, the imaginary point on the horizon at which receding parallel lines (used to create the illusion of **depth**) seem to meet, or vanish.

View The point from which the artist seems to have been looking in order to depict a **scene**.

Index of artists

Africa

    Côte d'Ivoire, Baule 14, 44

    Mali, Bamana 41, 46

Beckmann, Max 11, 44

Bourke-White, Margaret 21, 45

Brauner, Victor 5, 44

Cassatt, Mary 22, 45

Catlett, Elizabeth 17, 44

Cordier, Charles-Henri-Joseph 12, 44

Cornell, Joseph 37, 46

De Kooning, Willem 25, 45

Gogh, Vincent van 10, 39, 44

Gonzalez-Torres, Felix 32-33, 46

Hey, Jean (Master of Moulins) 36, 46

Hockney, David 18-19, 44

Homer, Winslow 23, 45

India

    Rajasthan, Jaipur 35, 46

    Uttar Pradesh 42-43, 46

Johnson, Eastman 18-19, 45

Klee, Paul 39, 46

Korea 32-33, 45

Lee, Doris 20-21, 45

Magritte, René 32-33, 45

Marshall, Kerry James 24-25, 45

Mexico (West), Nayarit 40, 46

Motley, Jr., Archibald J. 8-9, 44

Netherlands, The 26-27, 45

O'Keeffe, Georgia 38, 46

Peru (South Coast), Nazca 41, 46

Plaisted, Rebecca Stonier 32-33, 45

Seurat, Georges 30-31, 45

Sharaku, Toshusai 12-13, 44

Shukei, Sesson 18-19, 45

Snyder, Richard 34, 46

United States 21, 45

Wirsum, Karl 15, 38, 44

Wood, Grant 16-17, 44

Yu, Zhu 28-29, 45